EYE-ON ENERGY

Nuclear Power

ABDO
Publishing Company

Jill C. Wheeler

visit us at
www.abdopublishing.com

Published by ABDO Publishing Company, 8000 West 78th Street, Edina, Minnesota 55439.
Copyright © 2008 by Abdo Consulting Group, Inc. International copyrights reserved in all
countries. No part of this book may be reproduced in any form without written permission from
the publisher. The Checkerboard Library™ is a trademark and logo of ABDO Publishing Company.

Printed in the United States.

Cover Photo: AP Images
Interior Photos: Alamy pp. 5, 6, 12, 13, 14, 22; AP Images pp. 15, 25; Corbis pp. 7, 8, 9, 18, 19, 20;
    Getty Images pp. 4, 21, 29; Pebble Bed Modular Reactor (Pty) Ltd. p. 23; Peter Arnold p. 26;
    U.S. Department of Energy p. 16

Series Coordinator: Rochelle Baltzer
Editors: Rochelle Baltzer, Megan M. Gunderson
Art Direction & Cover Design: Neil Klinepier

Library of Congress Cataloging-in-Publication Data

Wheeler, Jill C., 1964-
  Nuclear power / Jill C. Wheeler.
      p. cm. – (Eye on energy)
  Includes index.
  ISBN 978–1–59928–807–9
  1. Nuclear energy–Juvenile literature. I. Title.

  TK9148.W53 2007
  621.48–dc22
                                                            2007007108

CONTENTS

TODAY'S ENERGY

People are using more energy than ever before. Rising populations and worldwide **economic** growth continue to increase energy usage. In fact, the International Energy Agency estimates the world's energy appetite will grow 65 percent by 2020.

Today, most of the world's energy comes from fossil fuels. These fuels are the products of resources such as coal, oil, or natural gas. To convert fossil fuels into energy, they must be burned. This process releases **carbon dioxide** into the atmosphere, which increases the risks of **global warming**. Also, fossil fuels are in limited supply. Scientists believe that someday the world will run out of them.

One alternative to fossil fuel energy is nuclear power. Unlike fossil fuel power

Most U.S. motor vehicles are powered by gasoline, which is a product of oil.

plants, nuclear plants do not release **carbon dioxide**. Currently, nuclear power provides about 20 percent of the electricity used in the United States. Other nations use it, too. France gets about 75 percent of its electricity from nuclear power. Worldwide, nuclear power supplies electricity to more than 1 billion people.

There are 103 commercial nuclear reactors operating in the United States.

ATOMIC POWER

Nuclear power was born from what scientists learned by creating the atomic bomb. In 1945, the United States dropped the first two atomic bombs used in warfare on Japan during **World War II**. More than 100,000 people died, and the war soon ended. Afterward, many people believed that using nuclear energy in positive ways could help make up for this loss. Thus began the age of nuclear power.

An atomic bomb blast is much more powerful and far-reaching than that from other explosives.

Both nuclear power and nuclear weapons obtain energy from splitting tiny particles called atoms. Nuclear power provides electricity to homes and businesses. It also fuels some submarines, surface ships, and spacecraft.

The world's first full-scale nuclear power plant began operating in England in 1956. The following year, the first large-scale nuclear plant in the United States opened in Pennsylvania. By 1979, there were 69 nuclear reactors operating in the United States.

However, things changed between the late 1970s and the mid-1980s. In March 1979, there was an accident at the Three Mile Island nuclear power station in Pennsylvania. A far worse accident occurred in April 1986 at the Soviet Union's Chernobyl (chuhr-NOH-buhl) station. After these incidents, popular support for nuclear power dropped dramatically.

One year after the Three Mile Island accident, people gathered to remember the event. Some of them protested against nuclear power.

CHERNOBYL

Many people consider the Chernobyl explosions the worst nuclear disaster ever. The Chernobyl power station is located near Pryp'yat, Ukraine, which was part of the former Soviet Union.

Early on April 26, 1986, a chain reaction went out of control. This caused an explosion, which started a fire that burned for nine days and led to more explosions. These events released several times more **radiation** into the atmosphere than the amount released by both atomic bombs dropped during **World War II**.

Winds sent radiation from the explosions in Ukraine throughout the world.

At first, Soviet officials pretended nothing had gone wrong. However on April 28, Swedish officials reported abnormally high levels of radiation. They demanded an explanation. Finally, the Soviet government admitted there had been an accident.

Radiation exposure and burns killed 32 people right away. Others died later from radiation sickness. Two thousand villages were torn down because of **radioactive contamination**.

Cleanup efforts lasted for three years. But surrounding areas continue to feel effects of the **radiation**. Around Chernobyl, many crops are still unsafe to eat. And, rates of **birth defects** and certain types of **cancer** are higher than average.

Much is still unknown about the accident's long-term effects. For years, Soviet leaders refused to provide correct information. So, researchers are still learning about the impact of the accident.

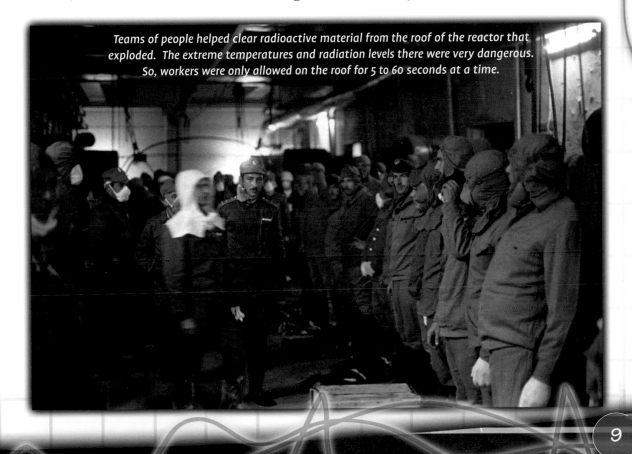

Teams of people helped clear radioactive material from the roof of the reactor that exploded. The extreme temperatures and radiation levels there were very dangerous. So, workers were only allowed on the roof for 5 to 60 seconds at a time.

NUCLEAR FISSION

Nuclear and coal power plants create electricity in similar ways. Both heat water to make steam. However, they produce the heat differently. Instead of burning coal, nuclear plants use a process called nuclear fission.

To understand nuclear fission, we must know a bit about atoms. Atoms are the basic unit of matter. Everything is made of them. They are extremely small and cannot be seen with the human eye. A strand of your hair is a million times thicker than an atom!

Inside an atom, there are even smaller parts. Its center, the nucleus, is the heaviest part. The nucleus contains protons and neutrons. Protons are positively charged, and neutrons have no charge. Electrons, which are negatively charged, circle the nucleus. The positive charge from the protons acts like a magnet. It keeps the negatively charged electrons inside the atom.

Nuclear fission occurs when an atom's nucleus is split into two lighter nuclei. This split releases an incredible amount of energy. It also releases neutrons. These neutrons cause other nuclei to split and release more neutrons, and so on. This chain reaction is the basic idea behind nuclear energy.

NUCLEAR CHAIN REACTION

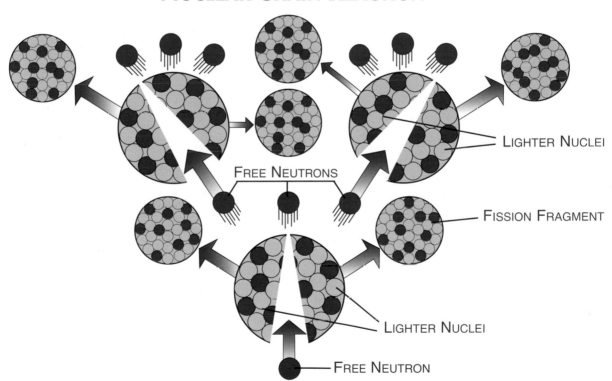

LIGHTER NUCLEI

FREE NEUTRONS

FISSION FRAGMENT

LIGHTER NUCLEI

FREE NEUTRON

Only certain atoms work well for nuclear fission. The atoms of a **radioactive** metallic **element** called uranium can be easily split and can sustain a chain reaction. Therefore, uranium can produce an enormous amount of energy from nuclear fission. In fact, one pound (.5 kg) of uranium can create the same amount of energy as 3 million pounds (1.4 million kg) of coal!

There are several natural **isotopes** of uranium on Earth. Uranium-238 (U-238) is the most common. The uranium-235 (U-235) isotope makes up less than 1 percent of Earth's uranium. For most nuclear reactors, U-235 is the only natural material that can be used to support a chain reaction. This is because it splits apart more easily than other uranium isotopes.

Before uranium can be separated, it is made into "yellowcake" at a mill.

After mining uranium, separating U-235 from U-238 is difficult and expensive. However, less than 5 percent of nuclear reactor fuel needs to contain U-235 to function properly. Therefore, the fuel consists mainly of U-238.

Miners use large machines to dig for uranium in
Wyoming. The state's uranium deposits account for
one-third of the total reserves in the United States.

INSIDE A REACTOR

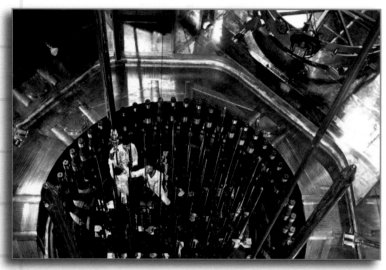

Workers at a nuclear power plant in Brazil step inside a nuclear reactor.

Controlled nuclear reactions take place inside a nuclear reactor. The three main parts of a reactor are the reactor vessel, the core, and the control rods.

The reactor vessel contains the main reactor parts. It has steel walls that are at least six inches (15 cm) thick and can contain high pressure. The core sits in the lower half of the reactor vessel. This is where fission takes place.

Inside the core, there are many fuel assemblies. Each assembly contains a bundle of fuel rods. A fuel rod consists of fuel pellets inside a metal tube. The pellets usually contain a powder form of uranium.

NUCLEAR REACTOR

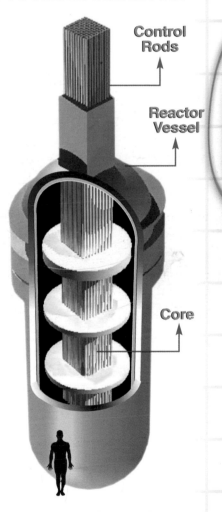

Control Rods

Reactor Vessel

Core

Control rods are located among fuel assemblies. These long metal rods regulate fission. When partly removed from the core, control rods start a chain reaction. When placed back into the core, they stop a chain reaction.

Most neutrons released during nuclear fission move too fast to cause fission in other U-235 atoms. So a moderator, usually water, is needed to slow them down. Water is also commonly used as a coolant. A coolant is necessary to absorb and transport the heat produced from a chain reaction.

MANAGING WASTE

Environmental and safety concerns have stalled the opening of a permanent nuclear waste storage site at Yucca Mountain in Nevada. The site is expected to open in 2017 at the earliest.

Eventually, fissioned uranium can no longer make chain reactions. It is then called spent fuel. Spent fuel must be handled very carefully. Nuclear fission makes fuel 2.5 million times more **radioactive** than it was originally.

Spent fuel is fatal. And, it can stay that way for thousands of years. After ten years out of a reactor, an unshielded spent fuel assembly still gives off deadly **radiation**. In less than three minutes, it would kill a person standing three feet (1 m) away.

The storage location for nuclear waste depends on its level of radioactivity. Low-level waste includes **contaminated** trash, gloves, and protective clothing. Such items lose radioactivity in 200 years and can be buried near the earth's surface.

Spent fuel rods are considered high-level waste, which can be **radioactive** for thousands of years. Plans are still being made for the disposal of this type of waste. Ideas include burying it under the ocean floor, storing it deep underground, or shooting it into space.

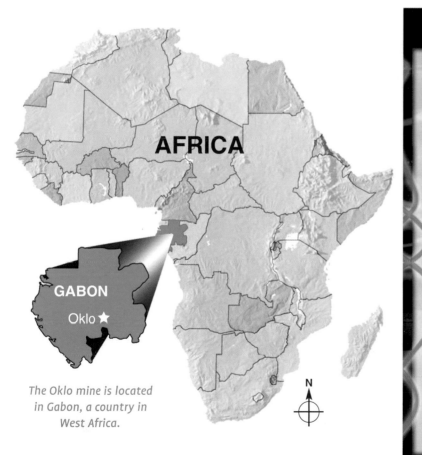

The Oklo mine is located in Gabon, a country in West Africa.

OKLO NATURAL NUCLEAR FISSION REACTORS

Inside a nuclear reactor, uranium is forced to produce fission. But uranium can also fission naturally.

In the early 1970s, scientists noticed that some uranium samples from a West African mine contained an unusually small amount of U-235. The only other uranium samples with similar levels of U-235 had already been fissioned in modern reactors.

Scientists concluded that about 1.7 billion years ago, natural conditions caused underground nuclear reactions at the Oklo mine site. Remarkably, the natural reactors were able to effectively contain radioactive waste.

Effects of nuclear fission from billions of years ago cannot be duplicated in a laboratory. So today, scientists study the Oklo natural reactors to learn more about permanently storing radioactive waste.

REPROCESSING

At France's La Hague reprocessing plant, spent fuel is cooled in a storage pool before reprocessing.

Standard reactors only use about 3 percent of the energy in nuclear fuel. Reprocessing reuses some of the spent fuel. Nuclear fission produces plutonium-239 (P-239), among other **radioactive isotopes**. Therefore, spent fuel must be separated in order to obtain the reusable materials.

However, reprocessing spent fuel is messy and expensive. It still produces waste that must be stored. And, P-239 is an ingredient for nuclear weapons. It is poisonous and extremely explosive.

Removing and storing P-239 increases the possibility that it will be used to make nuclear weapons. For that reason, some countries do not

La Hague is the world's largest commercial reprocessing site.

Plutonium is used to power spacecraft. Headed for Pluto, this spacecraft is powered by 24 pounds (11 kg) of plutonium.

allow the reprocessing of nuclear waste. Only France, Great Britain, Russia, India, and Japan reprocess spent fuel.

Nuclear power was born from the creation of nuclear weapons. Using waste from nuclear fission to make nuclear weapons remains a concern today. At the end of 2003, researchers estimated there was enough stored plutonium worldwide to make 40,000 nuclear weapons.

Countries that have nuclear power plants can choose to reprocess their spent fuel for weapons. That was how India made its first nuclear bomb in 1974.

In the early 2000s, Iran made world headlines because of its nuclear program. Iranian leaders said the program was for peaceful purposes only. But not everyone believed that. Some people feared Iranians wanted to be able to make nuclear bombs.

There is a risk even if a country does not want to make weapons. Thieves could steal reprocessed fuel and sell it. Many people worry that **terrorists** could make nuclear weapons in that way.

The International Atomic Energy Agency (IAEA) Board of Governors met at IAEA headquarters in Vienna, Austria, in March 2006. The board discussed fears that Iran continues to secretly work on building nuclear weapons. IAEA promotes safe and peaceful nuclear technology.

SAFETY CONCERNS

After the Three Mile Island and Chernobyl accidents, some people said nuclear power was too dangerous. But in recent years, **global warming** and rising oil prices have made it a considerable energy option.

Nuclear power supporters say that workers today know how to better avoid problems. In the United States in 1979, there were 2.1 accidents in the industry for every 200,000 hours employees worked. Today, there are 0.25 accidents per 200,000 hours.

There have also been changes in reactor design and construction. Passive reactors shut down on their own if something goes wrong. These reactors have safety controls that can eliminate reaction-produced heat. They also stop fuel and **radioactive** waste from escaping.

Nuclear power plant employees wear protective clothing to shield themselves from radiation.

Researchers are working on the next generation of nuclear reactors. Among these are fast reactors, which make their own fuel. They can use fission-produced **radioactive** materials as fuel. This avoids the need to permanently store such materials. However, fast reactors have **complicated** designs that are expensive to build. So far, they are only experimental.

A pebble-bed reactor holds about 330,000 uranium-filled pellets.

PEBBLE-BED REACTORS

Designed in Germany in the 1980s, the pebble-bed reactor is one type of passive reactor. Instead of fuel rods, this model uses graphite-coated uranium fuel pellets. About 10,000 tiny beads of uranium are inside each tennis-ball-sized pellet.

Instead of water and steam to transfer heat, pebble-bed reactors use a gas called helium. Helium cannot burn or become radioactive, which increases the safety of this type of reactor.

Each pebble produces a small amount of power. And, graphite absorbs heat. Therefore, it is impossible for temperatures to reach a high enough level to melt the core. But in the case of an accident, pebble-bed reactors would release very little radioactive material.

MODERN DESIGNS

Today's nuclear reactors can take advantage of advanced designs. For example, cooling systems have improved. Older systems use a series of pumps, pipes, and valves to push water through the cooling system.

Instead of a system with so many parts, some newer designs rely on gravity to push the water. These newer designs are smaller and have fewer moving parts. So, there are fewer things that could break.

However, there is a drawback to these designs. Smaller reactors produce less power. Yet they cost about the same as those that can generate more power. Many plant designers do not choose them for that reason.

Another new technology uses heavy water. A molecule of normal water contains two hydrogen atoms and one oxygen atom. Heavy water is made by replacing the hydrogen atoms with deuterium (doo-TIHR-ee-uhm) atoms. These atoms are twice as heavy as hydrogen atoms. Heavy-water reactors can use natural uranium as fuel and can be refueled during operation.

Scientists are also experimenting with using nuclear fusion as a power source. Nuclear fusion is the opposite of nuclear fission. Nuclear fusion happens when two light nuclei join to form a heavier nucleus. This process releases much more heat than fission and is easier to control.

In September 2006, Chinese scientists first successfully tested an experimental fusion reactor. In November, representatives from various countries, including the United States, signed an agreement allowing France to build a nuclear fusion reactor by 2040.

Nuclear fusion uses materials that are more plentiful than the uranium used in fission. The fuel does not contain materials that could be used to make bombs. And, nuclear fusion leaves much less **radioactive** waste. However, nuclear fusion is successful only under extreme pressure and in very high temperatures.

So far, such conditions cannot be safely constructed for commercial use. But in the future, nuclear fusion will most likely be a considerable energy source.

Nuclear fusion is the source of energy in stars.

OLKILUOTO 3 POWER PLANT UNIT

Finland is building the world's largest pressurized water nuclear reactor at Olkiluoto, an island in the western part of the country. This new reactor, OL 3, will join two other on-site operating nuclear reactors, Olkiluoto 1 and 2.

ENERGY CAPACITY: OL 3 will be able to produce 1,600 megawatts, which is enough energy to supply the needs of 1.8 million households.

TIMELINE: OL 3 is expected to begin generating electricity by 2009.

SAFETY: The reactor will have a concrete wall that is double-reinforced. The wall is designed to contain a meltdown of the plant's radioactive core and to withstand a hit from today's largest airplane.

WASTE STORAGE: Radioactive waste will be stored in a bedrock site 1,380 to 1,710 feet (420 to 520 m) below the earth's surface.

HIGHLIGHTS: OL 3 is the first new nuclear power station in Europe since the Chernobyl disaster. Its output alone will meet 10 percent of Finland's power needs.

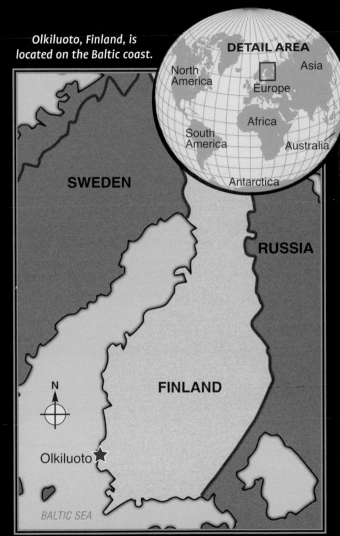

Olkiluoto, Finland, is located on the Baltic coast.

IN THE FUTURE

Rising oil and natural gas prices have turned the spotlight on nuclear power. And unlike oil, most uranium supplies are outside of politically charged areas such as the Middle East.

Yet nuclear power is expensive. When compared with coal or natural gas power, nuclear power costs up to twice as much to produce a **kilowatt-hour** of electricity. And, a new nuclear power plant costs about $3 billion.

The U.S. government supports the nuclear power industry in many ways. The industry receives **subsidies**. And, U.S. taxpayers help insure nuclear power plants against disasters. They also pay taxes to handle nuclear waste.

Nuclear power has an **environmental** cost, too. Nuclear power plants do not give off the **carbon dioxide** that coal or natural gas plants do. But there are still drawbacks. Mining and milling uranium burns fossil fuels, which creates pollution. And, building nuclear plants also requires fossil fuel energy.

FACT OR FICTION?

A coal power plant can release more radioactivity than a nuclear plant.

Fact. Sometimes coal has elements that release radioactivity when coal is burned. But when a nuclear plant is operating correctly, it keeps all radioactive materials contained.

Nuclear power plants have an average life span of 40 years. Three Mile Island's license to operate will expire in April 2014.

Most experts agree that nuclear power will be part of America's future. They believe it will be difficult to produce enough power without using it. In this case, more nuclear plants need to be built soon. It takes at least ten years to plan, approve, construct, and test a plant before it opens. Meanwhile, existing U.S. plants are nearing the end of their life spans.

GLOSSARY

birth defect - a physical or a biochemical abnormality present at birth. It may be inherited or caused by something that happens or exists in the environment.

cancer - any of a group of often deadly diseases characterized by an abnormal growth of cells that destroys healthy tissues and organs.

carbon dioxide - a heavy, fireproof, colorless gas that is formed when fuel containing the element carbon is burned.

complicated - having elaborately interconnected parts.

contaminate - to make unfit for use by adding something harmful or unpleasant.

economic - of or having to do with the way a nation uses its money, goods, and natural resources.

element - any of the more than 100 basic substances that have atoms of only one kind.

environment - all the surroundings that affect the growth and well-being of a living thing.

global warming - an increase in the average temperature of Earth's surface.

isotope - one of two or more atoms of the same element that have a different number of neutrons.

kilowatt-hour - a unit of electrical energy equal to the work done by one kilowatt, or 1,000 watts, acting for one hour. A watt is a unit of electric power that equals the work done at the rate of one joule per second.

radiation - the transfer of heat through matter or space in the form of waves or particles. Radiation sickness is a result of exposure to radiation. Common problems can include fatigue, nausea, and loss of teeth and hair.

radioactive - of, caused by, or showing radioactivity. Radioactivity is the rays of energy or particles given off when certain atoms of certain elements break apart.

subsidy - a government's grant to a person or a company to assist in an undertaking thought helpful to the public.

terrorist - a person who uses violence to threaten people or governments.

World War II - from 1939 to 1945, fought in Europe, Asia, and Africa. Great Britain, France, the United States, the Soviet Union, and their allies were on one side. Germany, Italy, Japan, and their allies were on the other side.

WEB SITES

To learn more about nuclear power, visit ABDO Publishing Company on the World Wide Web at **www.abdopublishing.com**. Web sites about nuclear power are featured on our Book Links page. These links are routinely monitored and updated to provide the most current information available.

INDEX